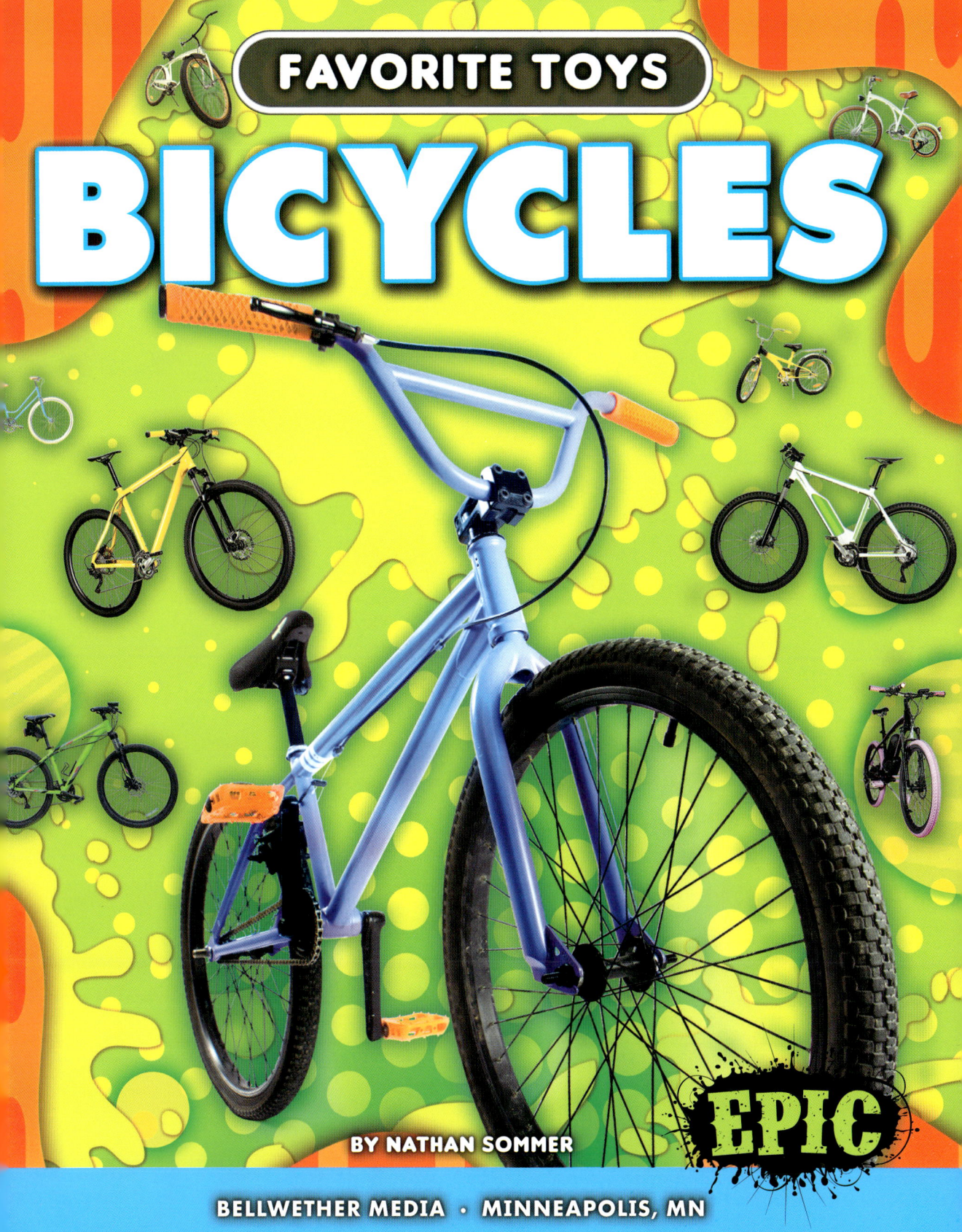

# FAVORITE TOYS
# BICYCLES

BY NATHAN SOMMER

EPIC

BELLWETHER MEDIA • MINNEAPOLIS, MN

# EPIC

Action and adventure collide in EPIC. Plunge into a universe of powerful beasts, hair-raising tales, and high-speed excitement. Astonishing explorations await. Can you handle it?

This edition first published in 2022 by Bellwether Media, Inc.

No part of this publication may be reproduced in whole or in part without written permission of the publisher. For information regarding permission, write to Bellwether Media, Inc., Attention: Permissions Department, 6012 Blue Circle Drive, Minnetonka, MN 55343.

Library of Congress Cataloging-in-Publication Data

Names: Sommer, Nathan, author.
Title: Bicycles / by Nathan Sommer.
Description: Minneapolis, MN : Bellwether Media, 2022. | Series: Epic. Favorite toys | Includes bibliographical references and index. | Audience: Ages 7-12 | Audience: Grades 2-3 | Summary: "Engaging images accompany information about bicycles. The combination of high-interest subject matter and light text is intended for students in grades 2 through 7"– Provided by publisher.
Identifiers: LCCN 2021044254 (print) | LCCN 2021044255 (ebook) | ISBN 9781644876350 (library binding) | ISBN 9781648346460 (ebook)
Subjects: LCSH: Bicycles–Juvenile literature.
Classification: LCC TL412 .S66 2022 (print) | LCC TL412 (ebook) | DDC 629.227/2-dc23/eng/20211004
LC record available at https://lccn.loc.gov/2021044254
LC ebook record available at https://lccn.loc.gov/2021044255

Text copyright © 2022 by Bellwether Media, Inc. EPIC and associated logos are trademarks and/or registered trademarks of Bellwether Media, Inc.

Editor: Elizabeth Neuenfeldt    Designer: Josh Brink

Printed in the United States of America, North Mankato, MN.

# TABLE OF CONTENTS

A Perfect Ride......................... 4
The History of Bicycles........... 6
Bicycles Today ...................... 14
More Than A Toy .................. 18
Glossary ............................... 22
To Learn More....................... 23
Index..................................... 24

# A Perfect Ride

A family rides bicycles along a trail. They speed past wildlife while exploring the woods.

Soon, they arrive at a beautiful lake. Bicycles helped them see so much in a little time!

# MANY RIDERS

Today, more than 47 million people ride bikes in the United States!

# The History of Bicycles

Bicycles were **invented** in Europe in 1817. They were wooden and had no **pedals**. In 1839, pedals were added.

Bicycles were not popular at first. Most were costly and unsafe to ride.

BICYCLE WITH NO PEDALS

PENNY-FARTHING BICYCLE

## ONE TALL RIDE

The penny-farthing bicycle was made in the 1870s. It had a large front wheel and a small back wheel. The front wheel was up to 5 feet (1.5 meters) tall!

# BICYCLE BEGINNINGS

**Starley's bicycle company, Coventry, England =** 🟣

Starley's bicycles were much safer. They were easier to **steer** and **brake**. The bicycles became very popular!

Bicycle **gears** were added in the late 1800s. These let riders control their speed.

BICYCLE GEARS

Kids and teenagers kept bicycles popular in the 1900s. By 1968, three in every four bicycles were sold to teenagers!

Tougher, faster bicycles were made next. **BMX bikes** were made in the 1970s for off-road racing and doing tricks. **Mountain bikes** first **debuted** in 1977.

Modern bicycle helmets were invented around this time. They kept riders safe.

BMX BIKE

# BICYCLE TIMELINE

**1817**
The first steerable bicycle is built

**1839**
Kirkpatrick Macmillan invents the bike pedal

**1885**
John Kemp Starley builds the safety bicycle

**1975**
Bell Auto Parts invents the modern bicycle helmet

**1977**
Joe Breeze creates the mountain bike

# Bicycles Today

There are many kinds of bicycles. **Road bikes** have thin tires and curved **handlebars**. Mountain bikes have strong **frames** for off-road riding. **Tandem bicycles** have more than one seat. They let two or more people ride one bike!

# BICYCLE TYPES

**road bike**

**mountain bike**

**cruiser bike**

**BMX bike**

Bicycles are popular among all ages. They have many uses. Some people ride them to school or work.

## THE LONGEST BICYCLE

THE LONGEST BICYCLE WAS MADE IN 2020. IT WAS OVER 155 FEET (47 METERS) LONG!

Riding bikes helps people exercise. Many families ride bikes to spend time together.

# More Than A Toy

Many people watch the Tour de France each year. This race covers around 2,200 miles (3,541 kilometers) over 23 days.

Others tune in to the X Games. Fans can see riders show off jaw-dropping tricks!

X GAMES

# TOUR DE FRANCE PROFILE

**What Is It?** A bicycle race between around 200 of the world's best male riders

**When Did It Start?** 1903

**Where Is It?** France and nearby countries

TOUR DE FRANCE

Bicycle fans visit Bicycle Heaven in Pittsburgh, Pennsylvania. This museum houses nearly 6,000 bikes!

Bicycles remain a favorite toy for kids and adults. They help people stay healthy and see the world!

# Glossary

**BMX bikes**—off-road bikes that are used for racing and doing tricks; BMX is short for bicycle motocross.

**brake**—to slow down or stop by using brakes; brakes are devices that slow or stop the movement of wheels on a bicycle.

**debuted**—were shown to the public for the first time

**frames**—the bodies of bicycles; the frame holds most of a bicycle's parts together.

**gears**—parts on bicycle wheels that can be moved to control speed

**handlebars**—bars riders hold onto that control a bicycle's direction

**invented**—made for the first time

**mountain bikes**—off-road bikes that have strong, lightweight frames and many gears

**pedals**—bicycle parts that riders push to move bicycles forward

**road bikes**—fast bikes with curved handlebars that are used for racing and exercising on paved roads

**steer**—to make a vehicle move in a certain direction

**tandem bicycles**—bicycles with at least two seats and two sets of pedals

# To Learn More

## AT THE LIBRARY

Abdo, Kenny. *Mountain Bikes.* Minneapolis, Minn.: Abdo Publishing, 2018.

Abdo, Kenny. *X Games.* Minneapolis, Minn.: Abdo Publishing, 2019.

Mikoley, Kate. *Tour de France.* New York, N.Y.: Gareth Stevens Publishing, 2021.

## ON THE WEB

**FACTSURFER**

Factsurfer.com gives you a safe, fun way to find more information.

1. Go to www.factsurfer.com.

2. Enter "bicycles" into the search box and click 🔍.

3. Select your book cover to see a list of related content.

# Index

beginnings, 9
Bicycle Heaven, 20
BMX bikes, 12
Europe, 6
frames, 14
gears, 10
handlebars, 14
helmets, 12
history, 6, 7, 8, 9, 10, 11, 12
mountain bikes, 12, 14
off-road, 12, 14
pedals, 6
penny-farthing bicycle, 7
Pittsburgh, Pennsylvania, 20
popularity, 5, 6, 9, 11, 16

profile, 19
road bikes, 14
safety, 6, 8, 9, 12
safety bicycles, 8, 9
sales, 11
Starley, John Kemp, 8, 9
tandem bicycles, 14
timeline, 13
Tour de France, 18, 19
tricks, 12, 18
types, 15
United States, 5
uses, 16, 17
wheels, 7, 8
X Games, 18

The images in this book are reproduced through the courtesy of: GROGL, front cover (hero); Berents, cover (top left); Eshma, front cover (top right, right bottom), back cover (all bicycles); Vladyslav Starozhylov, front cover (top left blue bicycle), pp. 2 (blue bicycle), 23; stockphoto-graf, front cover (left yellow bicycle, right ebike), pp. 15 (road bike), 22; MossStudio, front cover (left green bicycle); s_oleg, front cover (right yellow bicycle); Margo Harrison, p. 2 (black bicycle); Julian Rovagnati, p. 3 (red bicycle); Pressmaster, pp. 4-5; Print Collector/ Getty Images, p. 6; Hulton Archive/ Getty Images, p. 7; Science & Society Picture Library/ Getty Images, p. 8; Spiroview Inc, p. 9; H. ARMSTRONG ROBERTS/ Alamy, p. 10; Mirrorpix/ Getty Images, p. 11; Yesterdays Antique Motorcycles/ Wikipedia, p. 13 (Macmillan bicycle); Karen Roe/ Wikipedia, p. 13 (John Kemp Starley); Dubova, p. 14; Andrey_Popov, p. 15 (mountain bike); Tom Saga, p. 15 (cruiser bike); Gilang Prihardono, p. 15 (BMX bike); Irina Wilhauk, p. 16; Spotmatik, p. 17; NEALE HAYNES/ Alamy, p. 18; Radu Razvan, p. 19; MA PHOTOGRAPY, p. 19 (flag); P.Spiro/ Alamy, p. 20; Ecuadorpostales, p. 21.